ABUNDANCE BEYOND TRAUMA WORKBOOK

JEANNINE L. RASHIDI, AP

WORKBOOK

ABUNDANCE

BEYOND TRAUMA

Discovering Your Courage for Change and
Commitment to Yourself

JEANNINE L. RASHIDI, AP

CONTENTS

Claim your gift here: https://www.goodbyetension.com/contact -15 min. exploratory call to see what endless possibilities await you!

*If you are in a triggered state, go to the I'M TRIGGERED! Pocket guide at the back of this workbook for immediate relief. *

INTRODUCTION

Congratulations! The fact that you have picked up this workbook means you are curious to Discover your Courage by looking at the limitations your trauma has created in your life. You are about to begin a journey of Change by developing the most beautiful and Committed relationship with yourself where there is honesty and trust within.

I highly recommend you have a copy of <u>Abundance Beyond Trauma</u> to reference while using this workbook.

Additional worksheets can be found at the back of the workbook, giving you an abundance of opportunities to get to know yourself better through your healing journey.

What does it mean to be activated, charged, or triggered? When we perceive an unmet need or threat, this can create an emotional response known as a trigger response. When we have adverse life experiences or trauma, it's customary to be challenged or triggered by people, places, things, words, behaviors, smells, etc.

Have you ever been emotionally challenged or triggered by something or someone, and it takes hold of you in a way that seems unmanageable, leaving you in a fight, flight, or freeze response?

The Trigger Worksheet will help you process through a challenging experience or trigger to feel empowered instead of debilitated, creating a deeper relationship with yourself where there's honesty and trust.

It is essential to identify which part of you is triggered to give you a better perspective of your experience. Sometimes, it can be challenging to determine what you feel, so please refer to the *Feelings List*.

Reflecting on the experience to narrow down at what point you became triggered or activated will give you great insight to start healing. Since our experiences are related to our senses, the trigger will be connected there as well.

We perceive through our senses. What we perceive is ingested into our Emotional Heart and Mind and, depending on our past impressions, determines how well we digest what we have ingested.

What we see, hear, taste, touch, and smell are ingested through the senses, ready to be digested and interpreted. Instead, what happens in trauma or adverse experiences is a lack of digestive strength in perception.

The more you work through your triggers/activations, the better you will get to know yourself and the parts of you that have disconnected and are reliving the trauma time loops.

REMEMBER YOUR BREATH

Wherever the breath goes, the mind follows. Stay connected and aware of your breath as you begin working through your triggers.

The most powerful tool you have is your breath. It is also the most forgotten.

"If you train your mind to face its fears, you'll be utilizing your mind's sole purpose as a tool to use, not something that uses you."
\- Jeannine L. Rashidi, AP

THE TRAUMA-TRIGGER TIME LOOP COMMITMENT

Events that I witnessed or was directly involved in that were too much for my Emotional Heart and Mind/psyche to process led to a disconnect from my Emotional Heart and Mind, leaving parts of myself stuck in a time loop of the related event. The time loop gets activated when triggered, and the emotional, mental, and physical responses come from that part of me that's now reliving the adverse experience. I'm no longer in presence; I'm in the past and unable to see correctly as my lens of perception is from the stuck-triggered part of me. My actions and reactions may be confusing and immature to others and even to myself upon reflection.

During traumatic events, what tends to happen is a disconnection from the parts that are too much to bear, they become undigestible experiences, and those parts of me are disconnected and stuck in their time loops. Depending on the trigger that particular version will activate, the traumatic time loop will replay and unconsciously come through my thoughts, actions, behaviors, and beliefs.

Healing the trauma-trigger time loop is becoming aware of the disconnected and stuck parts—creating presence and awareness, as my Guardian/Higher Self, of those parts. I am befriending, taking full responsibility for these parts so that healing can happen. Once healing occurs, then integration between my Guardian/Higher Self and the disconnected aspect can merge and become one. I essentially become whole, unlocking more of my true essence and potential.

My reactions, feelings, and thoughts are clues to witnessing my disconnected aspects as they try to communicate with me and get my attention. If I am brave enough to see and listen, I will heal and integrate with them as I am the healer.

I will discover my courage to begin my healing.
I am committed to sticking with it.
I am open and ready to change.
I can only begin my journey from where I am.
I want an incredible relationship with myself!
________________________________/ ____/ ___ (Sign and date)

**INSERT AN IMAGE OF
YOURSELF HERE TO REMIND
YOU THAT YOU ARE IN
A RELATIONSHIP WITH
YOURSELF FIRST.**

CYCLES, PATTERNS, AND DISEASE
(Refer to Chapter 2)

"What if mental health is being comfortable enough in our body that we don't need to numb ourselves or escape from our feelings?"
Edan Harari

Experiencing or witnessing something horrifying or adverse can create a feeling of insecurity, fear, and intensity that's too much to process or digest mentally and emotionally, creating a split disconnect. What we think and feel can create ease or dis-ease within our entire being. It's circulating in our blood. In essence, there's a disconnect in the Heart and Mind channel, a divorce, if you will, within you, within the self - a continual pulling in opposite directions, leading to discord and even disease.

ARE THERE CYCLES YOU WOULD LIKE TO CHANGE IN YOUR LIFE?

List the cycles you are aware of:

1.

2.

3.

ARE THERE PATTERNS, THAT SEEM UNHEALTHY, THAT YOU WOULD LIKE TO CHANGE?

List the patterns you are aware of:

1.

2.

3.

DO YOU CURRENTLY HAVE DIS-EASE IN YOUR LIFE?

List all the dis-ease you are aware of:

1.

2.

3.

DO ANY OF THE CYCLES OR PATTERNS LISTED ABOVE SEEM TO CONNECT WITH THE DIS-EASE?

Which ones seem to connect?

1.

2.

3.

CAN YOU SEE YOUR CONTRIBUTION/ROLE IN THESE CYCLES, PATTERNS, OR DIS-EASES?

Describe:

Try using the Trigger Worksheet and then apply the EDHIR® process with all your listed cycles, patterns, and dis-eases to begin creating significant change in your life.

You are looking for the part of yourself that may feel like a victim, blaming others or believing that others have power over you. See if you can explore and discover the parts of you that have a belief that keeps this cycle, pattern, or dis-ease continuing. Notice if there is a disconnect when trying to connect with this aspect of you—work towards healing your Heart and Mind disconnect.

Should you need guidance or extra support, please reach out for a session online or in-person:
Goodbyetension.com
byetension@gmail.com
+1-408-372-7701

TRIGGER WORKSHEET

DATE:

TIME:

Describe the Triggering Moment:

WHERE IN MY BODY DO I FEEL THIS TRIGGER?
(REFER TO CHAPTER 7, IS YOUR BIG TOE TRIGGERED?)

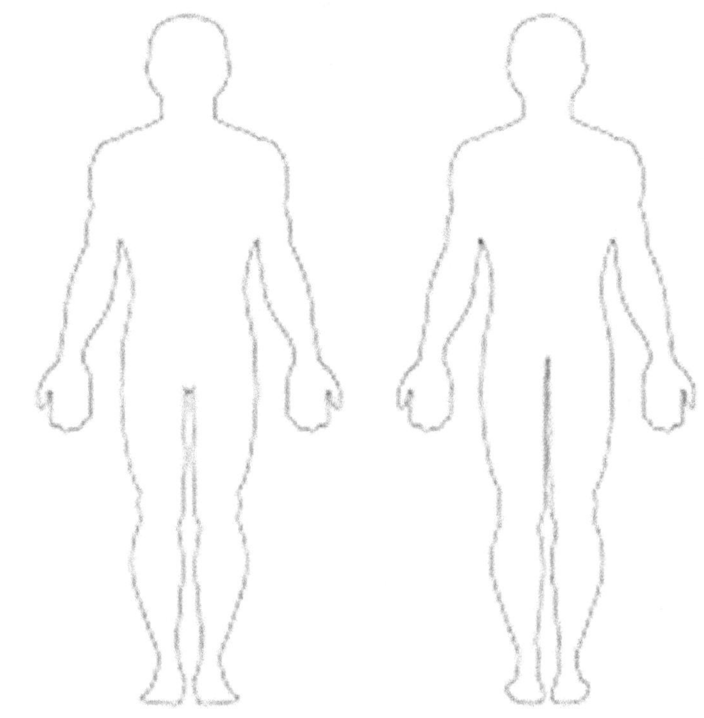

WHAT ARE THE FEELINGS I AM EXPERIENCING FROM THIS TRIGGER?
(REFER TO THE FEELINGS LIST.)

I feel______________, ______________________, __________________

DISCOVER THE EXACT MOMENT I GOT TRIGGERED.
WAS IT A....?

Word/Phrase: Person:
Look: Body Language:
Smell: Other:

I am Triggered by:

Follow steps 1-10 in the pocket guide at the back of the workbook or try applying the EDHIR® Process.

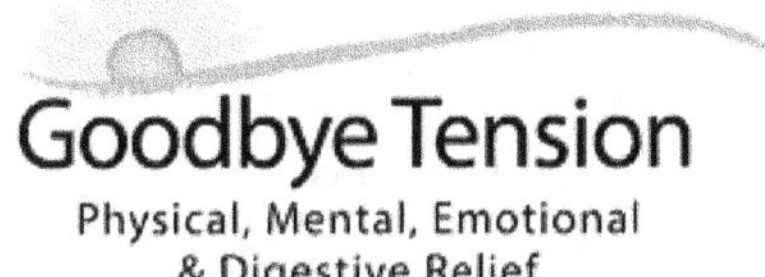

FEELINGS LIST

Angry	**Scared**	**Sad**
Hate	Weak	Lonely
Mad	Rejected	Hurt
Furious	Helpless	Unhappy
Frustrated	Confused	Regretful
Irritated	Insecure	Down
Rage	Anxious	Depressed
Jealous	Discouraged	Miserable
Hostile	Embarrassed	Sorrow
Skeptical	Foolish	Rejected
Selfish	Submissive	Guilty
Hurt	Rejected	Inadequate
Critical	Insignificant	Inferior

Peace	**Power**	**Joy**
Loving	Safe	Happy
Calm	Valued	Delightful
Thoughtful	Appreciated	Excited
Relaxed	Confident	Playful
Nurturing	Intelligent	Energetic
Content	Respected	Creative
Undisturbed	Secure	Satisfied
Sentimental	Important	Radiant
Harmonious	Resilient	Blissful
Soothing	Positive	Hopeful
Thankful	Self-Reliant	Grateful
Pleasant	Assured	Fulfilled

THE EDHIR® PROCESS
(Refer to Chapter 6)

Adhere: pronunciation **/əd'hir/ /əd'hɪr/**
Defined: to believe in and follow the practices of; to represent truthfully and in detail.

The process that allows you to be true to yourself

EXPLORE PHASE: STEP 1

The idea here is to dive deeper on an exploratory mission to see what you discover.

Find a comfortable place to sit, with your feet on the ground, and ideally, the spine is straight.

1. Connect with your breath by doing some <u>deep diaphragmatic breathing</u> for at least one full minute or more.

2. Close your eyes as you are going inward, connecting with deeper parts of yourself.

3. Bring awareness to every part of your body, beginning with your toes and moving slowly through the legs, thighs, and upwards to the pelvis.

4. Do a few squeezes, the equivalent of a Kegel squeeze for women, and for men, it's the type of contraction you would do if you needed to hold back your urine or gas.

DO NOT skip the squeeze, as this will ground you if you happen to feel like you are going out of your body.

5. Bring awareness from your pelvis, slowly tuning into every body part, moving up through the lower abdomen, back, belly button, and ribcage till you reach your heart, becoming aware of the sensations in the front and back of your precious heart. Notice if you are numb here or begin to feel something stirring and maybe even emotions.

6. Bring awareness from your heart, moving upwards to your throat, shoulders, arms, and hands, following the breath back up to your head, relaxing your forehead, and feeling your eyes sink back into their sockets. Feel the sensations and breath flow from the top of your head to the tips of your toes.

All the worksheets and exercises in this book ask exploratory questions.
The answers to these questions lead you to the next phase.
Try using your Trigger Worksheet or Known Triggers List as you explore.

DISCOVER PHASE: STEP 2

You'll now discover what's happening. Try to be open and not judge what you see, as all discoveries are acceptable. There's a part of you with a message. Once you discover the news, you'll be able to offer healing and change.

What is the story that has developed from this part of you that you discovered? Who is feeling a certain way about a specific experience? Maybe a past version or a younger version of yourself.

This story will lead you on a discovery mission leading to the next phase.

HEAL PHASE: STEP 3

You'll now offer that version of yourself everything needed to come out of the trauma time loop.

1. Embody/become/imagine that you are whatever archetype this part of you needs. Mother, Father, Guardian, Husband, Wife, Sibling, etc.

2. You will begin healing the disconnected part of yourself that you just discovered. Offering healing from the archetype that you are embodying. i.e., a small child may need the _ideal_ mother or father to offer love and safety. You will embody this _perfect_ archetype and essentially mother or father, the part of you that is a small child stuck in a trauma time loop.

3. You are essentially rewriting the story by coming in as the archetype to heal the trauma of that story. You may need to rescue that part of yourself.

4. Build trust between the archetype and the disconnected part of you stuck in the trauma time loop. This part of you may feel hurt, abandoned, rejected, etc. Since essentially a part of you disconnected from another part of you, abandoning & leaving that part behind.

5. Make a promise or commitment never to leave, hurt, reject, etc., that part of you again. You may need to convince this part of you that you are 100% committed. Be patient with yourself; this is the equivalent of going in for surgery and making sure the entire surgical procedure is complete before closing the surgical site. The next step cannot happen without this accepted commitment.

INTEGRATE PHASE: STEP 4

1. Look deeply into the eyes of the now healed part of you. Join hands and begin breathing in unison. Continue this until the two of you become one.

RELATE PHASE: STEP 5

1. You are now upgraded, and more of you is available. Now you will get to know this new you. Try to be as open-minded as possible as you may feel, think and be different. Others may need to adjust to the new you and

remember this can be triggering for others.

2. Create time each day to spend alone with yourself getting to know the new you. You are essentially dating yourself.

LET YOUR TRIGGERS BE YOUR TEACHERS

(Refer to Chapter 8)

The last thing you want to hear when you're triggered is that the person or event that triggered you is a blessing because it's pointing out that which is already inside you, which is an opportunity to apply the **EDHIR®** process to the trigger.

Adhere means to be true to, as in be true to yourself.

Let your trigger show you what's been hiding within. Have courage and commitment to yourself. What if you've been subscribing to a lie, and the trigger is trying to point out the lie? What if **EDHIR®** is your unsubscribe button?

Let's face it; You don't want to be triggered. Wouldn't you want to do anything to stop that experience? Wouldn't it be nice if that particular trigger stopped happening?

The only way to move forward is to be willing to see where you are.

You're triggered, have the courage and commitment to move forward, and not avoid yourself any longer.

Remember, the trigger is just pointing out that which has been inside you all along. It's a part of you, and avoiding it is no different than seeing you have an infected wound and pretending it doesn't exist. The wound continues to grow and fester and eventually leads to a more severe dis-ease. Doing the **EDHIR®** process is like pouring hydrogen peroxide on the wound, stitching it up, and bandaging it till it's healed. It stings at first, but it's better than leaving it infected.

IMAGINE WHO YOU WOULD BE IF YOU WEREN'T TRIGGERED.

Try that now; make a list of who you would be or what it would be like if you weren't triggered. Now take that list and post it everywhere in your home, computer screen, digital device, etc.; this will be your courage and commitment reminder to move forward and **EDHIR®** to your triggers.

Using the ***Known Triggers List*** is a great starting place to work with the **EDHIR®** process actively.

Yes, I'm suggesting you search for your triggers to get used to working through this process. This way, muscle memory is more likely to kick in when you get sideswiped by a trigger.

Practicing this is the equivalent of studying before an exam. If you've run through enough simulations, you'll have a more extensive skill set when the actual exam (trigger) happens. However, it is likely; you may not get triggered after you have gone through the **EDHIR®** process for each of your triggers/activations.

KNOWN TRIGGERS LIST

People:
1.
2.
3.

Places:
1.
2.
3.

Things:
1.
2.
3.

Behaviors:
1.
2.
3.

Other:
1.
2.
3.

What would it be like if I weren't triggered?

Who would I be without this trigger?

Accountability is super important. Find someone you trust to keep you accountable on your journey of courage and commitment toward maintaining loyalty to yourself by facing the illusion that your triggers create.

My accountability partners are:
1.

2.

3.

BREAKDOWN TO BREAKTHROUGH
(Refer to Chapter 9)

WHAT IF...

The most common fear-based thought, responsible for anxiety, distress, and the inability to move forward in life, is negative "What if" thoughts. The fear of what could happen is quite common for anyone with trauma.

The words we use possess energy; I'm always listening to what words others and myself are saying. I feel it's best to use the phrase Breakthrough instead of Breakdown. Why? Breakdown reminds me of what happens when your car stops working and needs to be fixed. A Breakthrough feels as if there's something on the other side you're about to discover. Doesn't that feel much more uplifting than needing to be fixed? I often feel like a rock layer is being chiseled away when I'm working through a trigger. Once the chiseling is complete, I breakthrough to a beautiful discovery of myself, a gift waiting to reveal itself, this is the motivation when you're at that fork in the road of the fight, flight, or freeze. What if you stayed and started chiseling? At the very least, you would be trying something other than the usual trauma response that you've become accustomed to. At best, you find the gift that's waiting to be revealed. If you can remember this during your most challenging times, you'll have outstanding success in your process.

Now you may be thinking, *If I work on _______________(fill in the blank), I'm afraid It will be too much, and I'll break down and never get up again.*

I get it, and I believed this for a long time myself. I decided to question this belief because it prevented me from moving forward in many aspects of my life. I used <u>The Work</u> by Byron Katie. I used part of her method by asking myself, "Is it true that I'll break down if I face __________?"

My response was, "Well, it's a possibility….." So, I went to the next question.

"How do I know for certain it's true?" Darn, I couldn't say for sure it was true. Now I needed to answer how it made me feel when I believed that I would break down. I felt terrified and defeated by this belief. The final question, who would I be without this thought? I wouldn't be afraid or defeated; I noticed that I felt stronger when I stopped believing that I would break down. So, I realized how much power this thought had over me and decided to cancel my subscription to that belief. I've been breaking through ever since.

Based on your responses to the **What If Worksheet**, you can see which side of the fence you're on, the fear side or the endless possibilities side. Both sides have an incredible amount of strength. The question is:

Are you where you want to be? _______________________

Do you want to be on the fear side? Of course, you don't, and maybe it's all you've ever known. But what if there were endless possibilities that motivate and excite you about your life on the other side? Go back to your worksheet and replace the negative, fear-based responses with a positive, motivating, continuous possibility response.

Take the first what-if and consider its endless possibility. How do you feel? Are you still on the fear side, or are you moving to the endless possibility side?

The idea is to change the thought pattern from negative to positive. For example, if the negative thought is, *"Why do I even try?"* The positive thought could be, *"I wonder what new things I'll learn today from trying?"* I prefer phrases that come from curiosity so that I am open to all possibilities.

The positive phrase could become your daily affirmation or mantra.

A mind is a tool that you use. As with any tool, it needs to be cleaned, sharpened, polished, etc. Otherwise, it becomes corroded and dull. This practice is cleaning up the corrosion.

WHAT IF WORKSHEET

What if...

Does this statement imply fear or endless possibilities?
(Refer to the positive/negative words list & feelings list)

Rewrite the statement from fear to endless possibilities.

Example: What if I don't succeed? Implies fear.
What if I am successful? Implies endless possibilities.

THE PERCEPTION OF FEAR

I love to use the acronym <u>F</u>ace <u>E</u>verything <u>A</u>nd <u>R</u>ise when I see the word "fear." This way, I'm essentially changing my relationship with fear.

The emotion of fear limits our ability to think, act, and perceive. That's not to say that the fear you experience when you face a life-threatening situation (i.e., a lion attacking you, a rapist, murderer) prevents you from thinking. On the contrary, that particular scenario and reaction keeps you alive. I'm referring to the perception of fear when there's no real danger; A trigger is fear. Thinking and acting from a triggered state is driven by fear.

The problem arises when we're unable to recognize when we're operating from a place of fear. The trigger is in the driver's seat, totally afraid and unable to think; this is where you need to call on your higher mind, higher heart, higher self, higher power, etc. The basic principle is to elevate from the triggered place. The first step to coming out of fear is acknowledging that you're in a fearful state and you need wisdom. Fear is the belief in something outside of yourself. Never forget your fearless self. The courageous and committed aspect of you that doesn't run away from fear or fight with fear but faces what you're afraid of, looking at it directly and discovering what's true.

The nature of the mind is continuous movement. Imagine you're in your favorite country and now your least favorite place. Now try not to think of either place. You see, in a split second, you could be in India and the next in Europe and then both. Unless you train the mind, its nature is to be anywhere and everywhere. If you train your mind to face its fears, you'll be utilizing your mind's sole purpose as a tool to use, not something that uses you.

Perception is how we interpret the input we're ingesting through our senses. How we interpret what we saw and what we felt becomes our perception. We hear, smell, taste, and analyze everything, which is how we perceive it.

Let's say you went on a late evening walk with a friend and noticed something on the ground in front of you. Your friend perceives it as a stick, while you perceive it as a snake. Since it's dark, you wouldn't know who was correct until more light or awareness came to the situation. This object, perceived as fear from one perspective and logic from another. As you grab your cell phone and turn on the flashlight, you see a stick. This object triggered the fear that was already inside. When you introduce light to dispel darkness or wisdom to dispel ignorance, the fear is observed as an imbalance in perception. Why did your friend have a logical response to the stick while you perceived it as a snake? Perhaps you were bitten by a snake when you grabbed a stick from a woodpile as a child. So, seeing a stick is a trigger for fear. Remember, fear limits and sometimes paralyzes your ability to think and act. The rational and objective part of the mind doesn't function as it is meant to because fear has taken over. Whereas the one who naturally perceived the stick as a stick didn't have an underlying fear trigger and, therefore, could use logic, reason, and deduction to assess that it was a stick.

MOVE FROM SURVIVING TO THRIVING

My mission in life is not merely to survive, but to thrive; and to do so with some passion, some compassion, some humor, and some style.
–Maya Angelou

A SURVIVING MINDSET JUST GETS BY.

Are you continuing to live, manage or exist despite the current or past danger or hardship?

Are the current relationships in your life supporting the surviving mindset? For example, continually identifying with your past trauma instead of moving beyond it.

A THRIVING MINDSET IS SEEING ALL THE ENDLESS POSSIBILITIES IN YOUR LIFE AND STRIVING TO REACH THOSE POSSIBILITIES, BELIEVING IN YOURSELF!

Are you prospering, feeling successful, growing, developing, and flourishing in your life?

Are the relationships in your life thriving?

What would it look like and feel like to be thriving?

CREATING YOUR INNER HOME

Realize that your world is only a reflection of yourself and stop finding fault with the reflection. Attend to yourself first, set yourself right, mentally and emotionally. The physical self will follow automatically.
-Nisargadatta Maharaj

By creating a sense of home internally, not only are you developing a relationship with yourself, but you're also making a safe space within. This is essential to the healing process for those who, while growing up or in unhealthy relationships, had unsafe homes or lived where there was no sense of individuality or boundaries. This is where you learn to trust yourself, provide for yourself, and take absolute full responsibility for yourself, including your happiness. It takes the dependency on others to make you happy off the table, creating space for interdependent relationships. Being at home within creates a stable internal environment that you're the master of. As you evolve with this concept, you'll notice that you're safe, secure, and positive internally, no matter the external circumstance.

Your ability to see clearly in times of chaos comes from the internal stability of being at home within.

How often do you try to fill up your day with to-dos?

Since I'm creating this workbook during COVID-19, this pandemic has created trauma and adverse life experiences for many of us. Suddenly, your to-do list regarding leaving your home became very limited. And you had no choice but to stay home with yourself, spouse or partner, children, family, etc. Anything that you may have been avoiding by being busy is now starring you in the face.

The ability to feel a sense of home within yourself is one of the most powerful tools.

When you have a sense of home within yourself, it doesn't matter where you live. It doesn't matter whom you live with. It doesn't matter whom you know. You always feel safe within yourself. The better sense of home you have within yourself, the higher quality of relationships you'll attract into your life because you won't be coming from a place of need.

Getting to know yourself when you're alone is profound as you may begin to notice an uncomfortable feeling, a need to keep busy, and distract yourself from this feeling. Have the courage to stay with this feeling to understand what is going on in your inner home truly. Turn on the lights, create safety and understanding and learn to believe and trust in yourself.

When you think of creating your home, of course, there's furniture, lighting, aesthetics, pictures, etc. and, the same thing happens when you're finding a sense of home within yourself. That means no matter what the external circumstances are, within you, you feel safe and supported, have a place to sleep, and have the nourishment that you need.

Try creating a time to work on feeling a sense of home within yourself. You can begin by doing the ***Creating Your Inner Home Worksheet.***

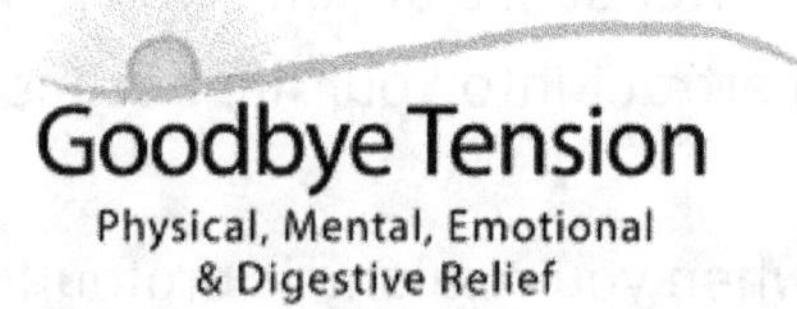

CREATING YOUR INNER HOME WORKSHEET

(Refer to Chapter 10)

What does a sense of home mean to me?

What are the boundaries that allow me to feel safe?

What does it feel like to be alone?

Is there a visual I can create within that reminds me of my safe space that is always with me?

Draw or insert your image here:

WORKING THROUGH INTENSE EMOTIONS

"When there is anger, there is always pain underneath
-Eckhart Tolle

ANGER is a messenger

Don't shoot the messenger! Anger is a signal arising deep from within that needs to be seen and heard so you can begin healing. It's easy to let anger run the show or even try to ignore it, but its power comes bubbling up like a volcano, eventually begging to be witnessed.

How do we honor and respect anger?

A part of you is trying to get your attention. Stop ignoring yourself. Honor and respect every aspect. You're incredible, and there's an intelligence that's trying to get your attention. Once you realize that anger is a messenger, you're more likely to be willing to take the journey of talking with your anger.

Create a safe space to explore this fierce emotion, an area where you can stomp your feet, scream (screaming into a pillow works), and write, or maybe you're brave enough to video your process to reflect on later. You'll need water to stay hydrated and tissue for crying. You may also want to include an old phone book that can be ripped and destroyed, giving anger an outlet. I suggest working with a practitioner if you feel that trying this out on your own is too intense. As you get familiar with anger, you'll become comfortable with it as it comes.

If you live with others, let them know you're about to explore some intense emotions or go into a healing session, and there may be loud sounds. They don't need to worry; however, give them an idea of when they should come to check on you, especially if this is something new that you're exploring.

Now that you're ready let's explore the Who, What, When, Where, and Why of your anger.

EXPLORE YOUR ANGER WORKSHEET

Who or what triggered the anger reaction?

What does anger want to say? Record it or write it down as you express it.

What words or interactions allowed anger to present itself?

Where do you feel anger? Scan your body from your big toe to your head if you're unsure.

Is there a past memory of being this angry? Try to get to the most intense and earliest memory.

Have you ignored a part of yourself? Consider that you may have ignored a feeling of sadness or fear before the anger messenger showed up.

Often, the feeling of sadness or fear is hiding behind anger. Anger is the messenger trying to point out the deeper sadness or fear. Sadness needs the flow of tears to open the heart, and fear needs to be seen. When either of these is ignored, then anger shows up with a message to be heard.

Are you doing what you've been told you should do, instead of checking to see if that's true for you?

When you do things, you have been told you "Should do" without questioning it, you may end up feeling violated and *shoulding all over yourself!*

Are there boundaries or other wisdom that needs to be honored?

When you do not question situations, actions, etc., and truly check in with yourself, you may end up feeling that your boundaries have been violated. You violate yourself when you do not check in before making decisions.

"I discovered that when I believe my thoughts I suffered, but when I didn't believe them, I didn't suffer, and that this is true for every human being. Freedom is as simple as that."
-Byron Katie

The Fear I ignored is:

I looked at my fear directly and asked:
Is it true?

How do I know for certain it's true?

How do I react when I believe this thought?

Who would I be without this belief/thought?

See The Work by Byron Katie

I acknowledged my sadness of:

I allowed myself to cry and open my heart channel.

After a good cry I feel:

My messenger of anger pointed out ____
____
Showing up in the ____part of my body.
I ignored the signal of fear/sadness (circle one) when__________________________
____
I learned ____
____
I am committed to listening to the signals of fear, sadness, anger and honoring their wisdom ____ (Sign/date)

MOVING THROUGH FIGHT, FLIGHT AND FREEZE RESPONSES

I'm sure you can remember a moment when every part of you wanted to get away from or out of a situation. Depending on the dominating quality behind this energy, you'll either fight, flee, or freeze. What if we could learn to move with this energy and intensity with more awareness?

How can you use movement and awareness when you're aware that fight, flight, or freeze is happening?

You need the opposite quality to change a habit that has also become ingrained. The fight, flight, or freeze response is incredibly powerful. Your heart rate and blood pressure increase, your blood flow is being redirected, you may have pale or flushed skin, pupils will dilate to bring in more light, and the sensation of pain may be reduced until you feel safe again. The senses become heightened as you see and hear things you may not usually notice, creating a feeling of being on edge. Your memory can be affected from clear and vivid to a complete blackout of the incident; You may be tense or trembling since stress hormones circulate throughout your body. Your bodily functions may be affected, which aligns with the phrase, "He scared the crap out of me." All jokes aside, this experience is quite visceral, and we're designed to have this response to protect ourselves from grave danger.

With trauma, we perceive a threat when there's most likely no danger; therefore, we need to go back and question those triggers to reduce the power of the belief that there's a life-threatening danger when there is none.

The body naturally will move during a fight or flight response, so the idea here is to become more aware of that movement and consciously direct it instead of being taken over by it. Try to make movement more conscious, so you're less likely to move unconsciously. I use the imagery of a lion about to pounce. Do you want to be the lion that pounces before it realizes its surroundings (that wouldn't be a wise lion), or do I want to be the lion moving with intelligence? If you've ever watched a lion in the wild, they move with intention only once they have observed their prey and the surrounding threats, and then they wait. I'm not preparing you to pounce; I'm showing you your animal instinct.

If you have healthy people in your life who support your healing, you can always tell them the new things you might try during your triggers to come out of them quicker. If not, no worries; you're working toward becoming your own best friend.

FIGHT RESPONSE

Step 1: Breathe. Wherever the breath goes, the mind follows.

Step 2: Acknowledge that you're in a fighting triggered space.
The power of seeing something as it is is profound.
Start by opening and closing your hands to bring more awareness vs. the closed fist that may happen when preparing for a fight or even running away. If you've been living with your triggers for some time, I'm sure you're already aware of the thoughts and behaviors during this time. The more awareness you create, the less charge the trigger will have over you. Next, roll your shoulders like a boxer preparing for his fight. To clarify, you're not preparing for a fight; you're preparing for presence and the ability to resist the fight response. Next, move your head, stretching both sides of your neck, and take 7 big, deep breaths before acting on any feeling. Remember where the breath goes, the mind follows. Finally, try to notice your thoughts. Just observe them. Do not judge them or act on them.

Step3: Ask for a pause or time out from the situation.

Step 4: Explore yourself. Meaning look at what your current state is.

When did my state of being shift?

Which sense became activated?

Was it something that was said?

Was it a look?

Was it body language?

Was it a smell?

Keep moving if you're still feeling the fight; this is a great practice to move and ask yourself these questions.

Step 5: Discover all parts of you to see what happened inside of you. Often a fight has to do with feeling threatened (fear) or feeling angry. There might be sadness or fear behind this anger.

Remember, the other person involved only triggered that which was already inside of you. So if you're pointing the finger, then look at the other three pointing back at you.

What are the three fingers pointing out? 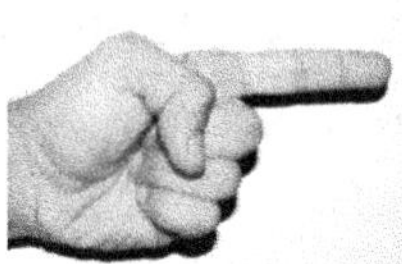

1. This trigger is your teacher.
2. Question your thoughts, beliefs, and actions at this moment.
3. Face Everything And Rise (F.E.A.R)

Being willing to face yourself and rise above the fight is where the real power is. Pointing the finger and not looking at yourself is a fear response.

My fight responses / thoughts are:

Imagine Water representing flow and/or Earth representing a solid & stable ground. Bravely change your inner dialogue to reduce the fight response.

My brave inner dialogue says: (look for the opposite quality of the previous question.)

My promise/commitment to this part of me is:

Step 6: Heal. Healing can now begin. Take all that you've discovered and start giving that part of you that's triggered, having a fighting response, the wisdom, compassion, and love needed to become whole. Again, look for the required archetype for this healing, Mother, Father, Guardian, etc.

Step 7: Integrate. Once healing has happened, you can now integrate-join with the disconnected part of you to become more whole. The triggered version of you was disconnected and stuck in a time loop of memory from the past. Once you heal that aspect, you naturally integrate and become one with this aspect of yourself.

Step 8: Relate. You're now an upgraded version of yourself, having integrated with the disconnected aspect. You must get to know yourself with this integration. Take yourself on a date!

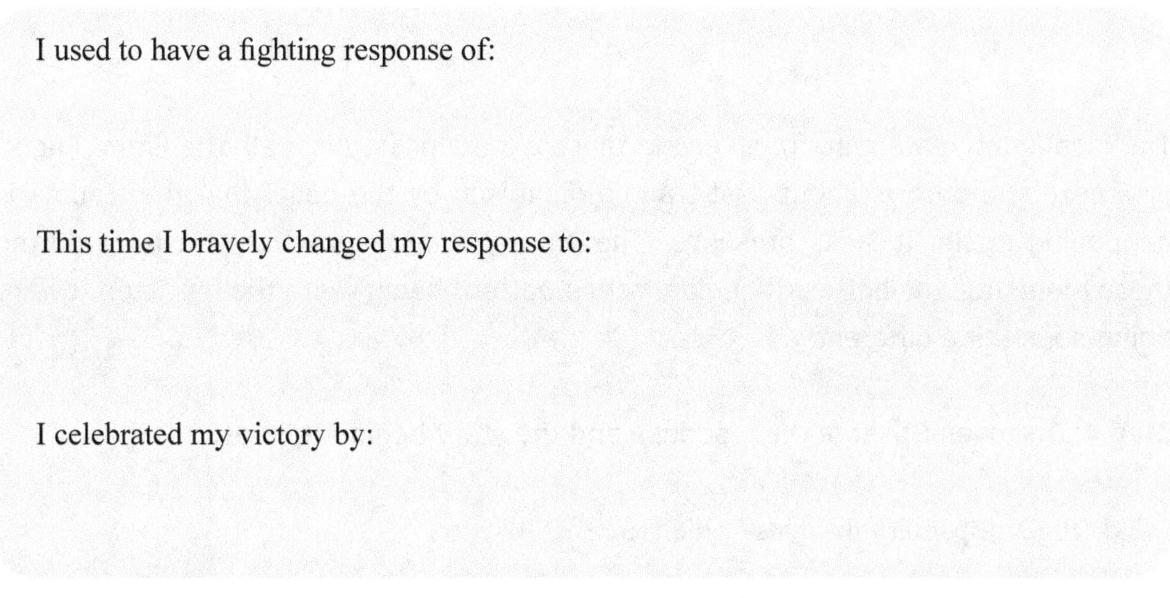

I used to have a fighting response of:

This time I bravely changed my response to:

I celebrated my victory by:

FLIGHT RESPONSE

The Flight response is characterized by an uncontrollable urge to run away from a situation, avoid something or someone. Usually, the emotion is Fear.

Step 1: Take a few deep breaths and notice how the body wants to move away.

Step 2: Try moving from side to side, putting all your weight on one leg and then the next. This way, your body is moving with that energy.

Step 3: Explore-Ask yourself the following questions:

1. Why do I want to run away?

2. What's the perceived threat?

The idea is to create more presence in these experiences. After all, the Fight, Flight, or Freeze response is about past trauma disguised by the belief that the trauma is happening again. It lacks presence. The more presence practice you have during these moments, the better. Changing from a pattern begins with the first step toward doing something different.

Step 4: Discover-Observe the response and the story behind this response.

My flight responses / thoughts / beliefs are:

Step 5: Heal-Offer the part of you that is scared, wanting to run away, everything they need. Safety, compassion, understanding, and a promise to always be there and never leave, hurt, abandon, etc.

The part of me that is scared needs:

My promise/commitment to this part of me is:

Step 6: Integrate by looking deeply into the eyes of the version of you that just healed, hold hands, and breathing together until the two of you become one.

Step 7: Relate by taking time to get to know yourself now that you are more integrated and whole. This is a special time of curiosity. Who are you now?

FREEZE RESPONSE

The freeze response is fascinating because you literally feel as if you're frozen or stuck and can't move.

Step 1: Connect with your breath. The deeper the breaths, the more movement is happening internally to support you in coming out of the freeze.

Step 2: Move your eyes around, left to right, right to left, up and down, circle toward the right, and then the left.

Step 3: Identify three things in the space you're in to bring presence to this moment. Preferably three living things representing life and nature since we're connected to nature, and consciousness within nature supports being present.

Step 4:
- Begin to move.
- Maybe swing your arms.
- Move your legs.
- Wiggle your toes and fingers.

Any movement is helpful to unfreeze. Once you can move, you could try an inner dialogue.

Step 5: Explore what made you freeze.

Was it a sound?

Someone?

Something I saw?

Smell?

Other?

Once you've Discovered what made you freeze from the questioning in step 5, you can move on to the Healing of that version of you that had a past response to a current situation. Usually, it's the version of you that experienced that particular trauma.

Step 6: Discover

What is the story from the version of me that froze?

Step 7: Heal

I healed this part of me by giving myself:

My promise/commitment to this part of me is:

Step 8: Integrate by looking deeply into the eyes of the version of you that just healed, hold hands, and breathing together until the two of you become one.

Step 9: Relate by taking time to get to know yourself now that you are more integrated and whole. This is a special time of curiosity. Who are you now?

DAILY ROUTINE AND SELF-CARE

(Refer to Chapter 14)

Ayurveda is the science of life that originated in India over 5,000 years ago. We are directly connected with the rhythm of nature and the five elements, and when the natural rhythm becomes disrupted, the elements become imbalanced, and disease happens. But, on the other hand, creating a balanced and harmonious rhythm creates a strong foundation for health.

The path of health and wellness is determined by your lifestyle, routine (Vihara), and your inputs (Ahara).

The five key ingredients for stability using the ancient wisdom of Ayurveda are:

1. Lifestyle and routine.
2. Perception
3. Breath
4. Food
5. Water

Your lifestyle and routine rhythm are set based on your sleep cycle. When you sleep determines when you wake, when you eat, your ability to use all your faculties, and your ability to take care of yourself.

Sleep is the mind at rest. At certain times of day, the elements are at their strongest; Pitta, the energy of transformation and digestion is from 10 pm to 2 am and from 10 am to 2 pm.

Mental digestion happens when the mind is at rest during sleep from 10 pm to 2 am. This is very important for everyone to maintain a healthy rhythm and balance. For those of us who've had trauma and adverse life experiences, it's critical to have a consistent sleep pattern that begins at or before 10 pm so that all the undigested mental and emotional impressions and experiences can start digesting.

Good sleep hygiene includes:
- Turning off all digital devices an hour or more before bed
- Calming breath practices such as deep diaphragmatic or alternate nostril breathing
- Dimmed lights an hour before bed
- Relaxing music

WHAT HAPPENS WHEN YOU MISS THE MENTAL DIGESTION HOURS OF 10 PM TO 2 AM?

You may get a burst of energy, allowing for more tasks to be done, staying up into the wee hours of the morning. Many people refer to themselves as "Night Owls" for this reason. This burst of energy comes at a cost eventually. Our body rejuvenates and repairs during sleep; sleep is the mind at rest, and the mind needs to digest. Many long-term imbalances come from improper sleep habits.

Some of these imbalances include:
- Memory issues
- Trouble with thinking and concentrating
- Accidents
- Mood changes
- Weakened Immunity
- Weight gain
- High blood pressure
- Risk for Diabetes
- Risk for Heart Disease
- Low sex drive

Fill out the ***Daily Self-Care Tracker*** to start creating more awareness around your current routine and making gentle adjustments to create balance.

DAILY SELF-CARE TRACKER

DATE: **I WOKE AT:**

UPON WAKING I FEEL...

Breathing Practice	**Movement Exercise**	**Breakfast**	**Water**
Type:	Type:	When:	Quantity:
How long:	How long:	What:	Temp:

What was the best part of the morning?

How would I have preferred the morning been?

What can I change within for a better experience?

MID-DAY I FEEL....

Breathing Practice
Type:

How long:

Work/Study

Lunch
When:

What:

Water
Quantity:

Temp:

What was the best part of the afternoon?

How would I have preferred the afternoon been?

What can I change within for a better experience?

EVENING I FEEL...

Breathing Practice
Type:

How long:

Chores

Dinner
When:

What:

Water
Quantity:

Temp:

What was the best part of the evening?

How would I have preferred the evening been?

What can I change within for a better experience?

Did I resolve my emotions, experiences, & perceptions using the EDHIR® process or the I'm TRIGGERED! Pocket guide?
Explain:

PREPARING FOR SLEEP I FEEL...

Breathing Practice	**Self-Care**
Type:	Type:
How long:	Went to sleep at:

CONCLUSION

At the end of the day, you have to live with yourself. Your choices, actions, decisions, thoughts, feelings, etc. Making yourself a priority takes great courage. Remember that!

The purpose of this workbook was to help you become more aware of the disconnected parts of you. Take time every day to check in with yourself, and you will find that you are becoming more aware and connected.

Key points to remember to keep a healthy balance in mind, emotional heart, and body

1. Where ever the breath goes, the mind follows.
2. Create a 5 min—breathing practice morning and evening.
   - Deep Diaphragmatic
   - Brahmari (humming)
   - Alternate nostril breathing
3. Create a consistent routine for sleeping around the 10 pm hour.
4. Eat around the same time, morning, noon, and evening.
5. Create space and time to look at your triggers and activations.
6. Identify your feelings and work through them.
7. Stay big as your higher-self aspect while doing your inner healing work.
8. Ask for help when you need it.
9. Turn judging yourself into loving yourself.

Use the I'm TRIGGERED! Pocket Guide for immediate support and the EDHIR(R) process for the inner healing work.

You are a courageous healer!

I'M TRIGGERED! POCKET GUIDE

Step 1: Stop.

Don't make decisions!

Excuse yourself or ask for a time out (self-responsibility is very empowering).

BREATHE with 2 short inhales and 1 long exhale.

Step 2: Locate

Locate three objects, preferably that are related to nature or that represents the current time and space.

Keeping the eyes moving creates a presence that can reduce the reactive fight, flight, or freeze response.

BREATHE with 2 short inhales and 1 long exhale.

Step 3: Identify

Identify your well-wishers-helpful people.

Giving the mind the remembrance of allies is positive, which may counteract the negative experience.

BREATHE with 1 long, slow, deep inhale, and a slow exhale.

EDHIR (R)

Step 4: Explore

What's the primary feeling you're having?

(Write it down, so you don't get distracted by your mind maze)

If you use your smartphone, this will create a timestamp for the note, which is excellent for tracking patterns.

BREATHE with 1 long, slow, deep inhale, and 1 slow exhale.

Step 5: Discover

Identify your trigger down to the simplest form.

Was it a smell, sound, taste, thought, word, touch, something you saw, or body language? (Write it down)

BREATHE with 2 quick inhales and 1 slow exhale.

Step 6: Get Big

Get big, real big. Imagine you're so big that you have a 360-degree view of the part of you that's triggered.

You're now the Guardian of that triggered aspect. At first, it's helpful to imagine a big you and a small you.

BREATHE with long, slow inhales and exhales.

Step 7: Heal

As you witness the triggered, small version of yourself feeling _________triggered by _______., What wisdom and healing does this version of you need?

How can you offer safety and security so that the higher wisdom from the Guardian or big you will be heard by the small you?

You're essentially building trust with this aspect of yourself and taking full guardianship, which includes showing them a bigger picture, a different perspective with the love and protection they need to feel safe.

Remember to make them a promise that you're taking full responsibility and won't abandon them. If you miss this step, it may be difficult for integration to begin.

BREATHE with long, slow inhales and exhales.

Step 8: Integrate

Healing has happened, and it's time to integrate the disconnected, healed aspect with the present and evolved version of yourself.

BREATHE deeply as you observe this union happening.

Step 9: Test

Imagine you're back in the place where you began, triggered by_________ and feeling_______.

Do you get triggered by this?

If yes, repeat steps 1-8. If not, move to step 10.

Step 10: Relate

This is where you get to know the upgraded version of yourself.

You tested your work and upgraded from being triggered to being empowered.

You may relate differently, be open to possibilities, and try not to put limitations on yourself.

Take yourself on a date to get to know the new you.

Congratulations, you did it. CELEBRATE!!!!!

EXTRA WORKSHEETS

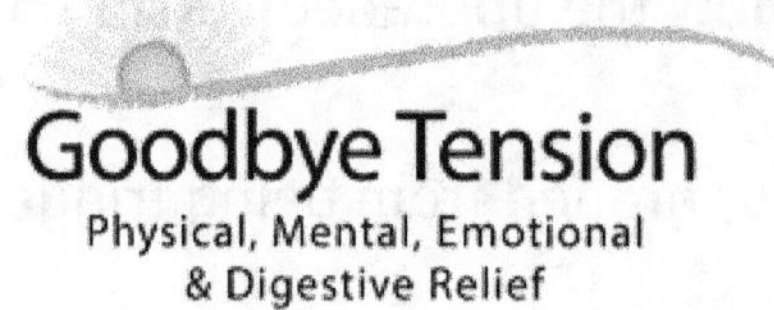

TRIGGER WORKSHEET

DATE: **TIME:**

Describe the Triggering Moment:

WHERE IN MY BODY DO I FEEL THIS TRIGGER?
(REFER TO CHAPTER 7, IS YOUR BIG TOE TRIGGERED?)

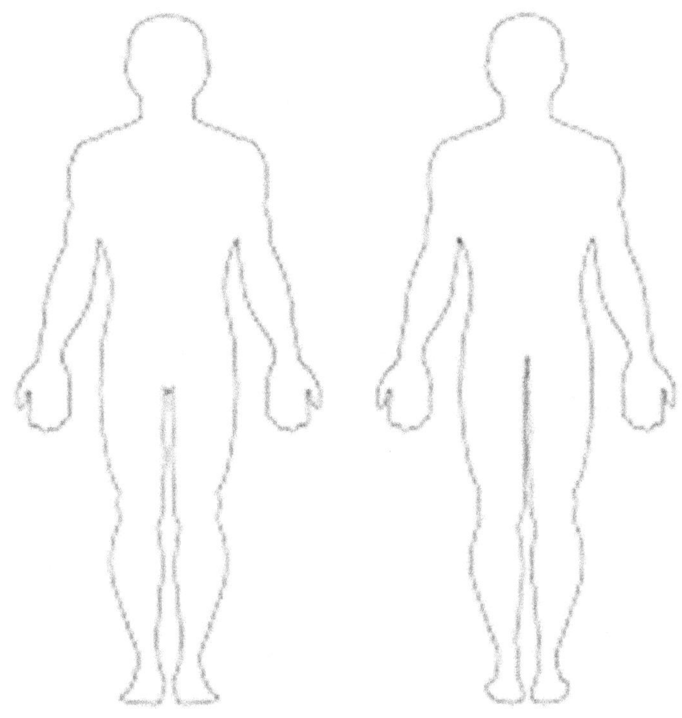

WHAT ARE THE FEELINGS I AM EXPERIENCING FROM THIS TRIGGER?
(REFER TO THE FEELINGS LIST.)

I feel________________, ____________________, ___________________

DISCOVER THE EXACT MOMENT I GOT TRIGGERED.
WAS IT A....?

Word/Phrase: Person:

Look: Body Language:

Smell: Other:

I am Triggered by:

Follow steps 1-10 in the pocket guide at the back of the workbook or try applying the EDHIR® Process.

TRIGGER WORKSHEET

DATE: **TIME:**

Describe the Triggering Moment:

WHERE IN MY BODY DO I FEEL THIS TRIGGER?
(REFER TO CHAPTER 7, IS YOUR BIG TOE TRIGGERED?)

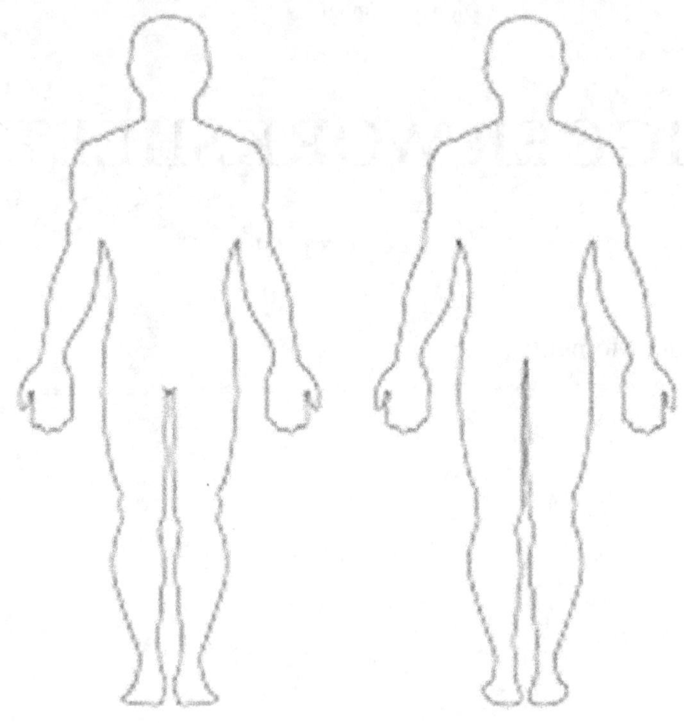

WHAT ARE THE FEELINGS I AM EXPERIENCING FROM THIS TRIGGER?
(REFER TO THE FEELINGS LIST.)

I feel_______________, _______________, _______________

DISCOVER THE EXACT MOMENT I GOT TRIGGERED.
WAS IT A....?

Word/Phrase: Person:

Look: Body Language:

Smell: Other:

I am Triggered by:

Follow steps 1-10 in the pocket guide at the back of the workbook or try applying the EDHIR® Process.

TRIGGER WORKSHEET

DATE: **TIME:**

Describe the Triggering Moment:

WHERE IN MY BODY DO I FEEL THIS TRIGGER?
(REFER TO CHAPTER 7, IS YOUR BIG TOE TRIGGERED?)

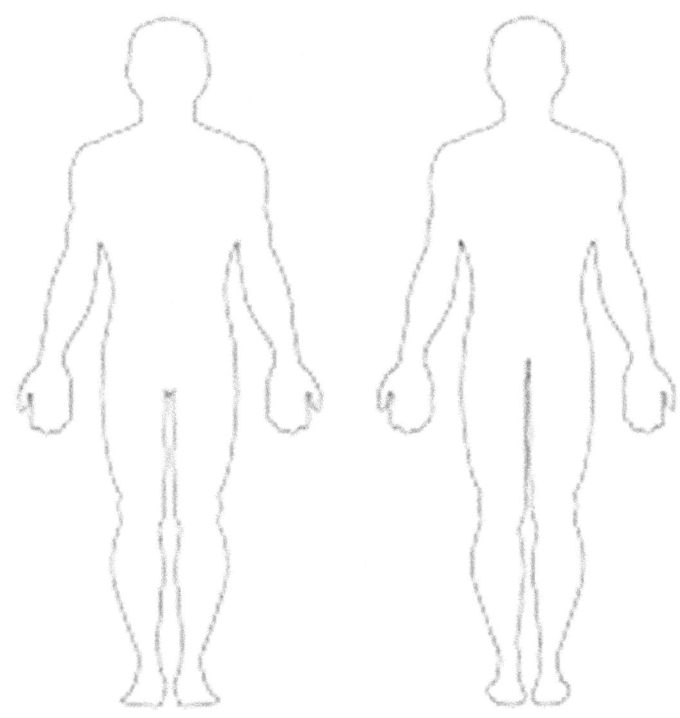

WHAT ARE THE FEELINGS I AM EXPERIENCING FROM THIS TRIGGER?
(REFER TO THE FEELINGS LIST.)

I feel_______________, _______________, _______________

DISCOVER THE EXACT MOMENT I GOT TRIGGERED.
WAS IT A....?

Word/Phrase: Person:

Look: Body Language:

Smell: Other:

I am Triggered by:

Follow steps 1-10 in the pocket guide at the back of the workbook or try applying the EDHIR® Process.

WHAT IF WORKSHEET

What if...

Does this statement imply fear or endless possibilities?
(Refer to the positive/negative words list & feelings list)

Rewrite the statement from fear to endless possibilities.

Example: What if I don't succeed? Implies fear.
What if I am successful? Implies endless possibilities.

WHAT IF WORKSHEET

What if...

Does this statement imply fear or endless possibilities?
(Refer to the positive/negative words list & feelings list)

Rewrite the statement from fear to endless possibilities.

Example: What if I don't succeed? Implies fear.
What if I am successful? Implies endless possibilities.

WHAT IF WORKSHEET

What if...

Does this statement imply fear or endless possibilities?
(Refer to the positive/negative words list & feelings list)

Rewrite the statement from fear to endless possibilities.

Example: What if I don't succeed? Implies fear.
What if I am successful? Implies endless possibilities.

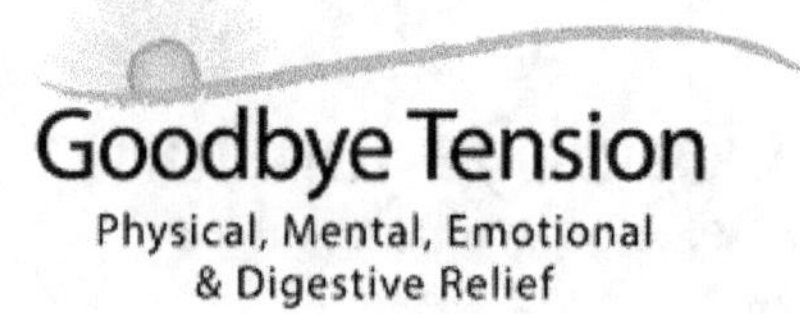

CREATING YOUR INNER HOME
WORKSHEET

(Refer to Chapter 10)

What does a sense of home mean to me?

What are the boundaries that allow me to feel safe?

What does it feel like to be alone?

Is there a visual I can create within that reminds me of my safe space that is always with me?

Draw or insert your image here:

CREATING YOUR INNER HOME
WORKSHEET

(Refer to Chapter 10)

What does a sense of home mean to me?

What are the boundaries that allow me to feel safe?

What does it feel like to be alone?

Is there a visual I can create within that reminds me of my safe space that is always with me?

Draw or insert your image here:

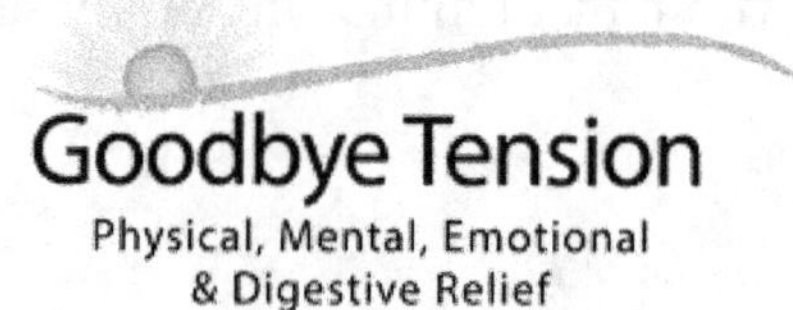

CREATING YOUR INNER HOME WORKSHEET

(Refer to Chapter 10)

What does a sense of home mean to me?

What are the boundaries that allow me to feel safe?

What does it feel like to be alone?

Is there a visual I can create within that reminds me of my safe space that is always with me?

Draw or insert your image here:

EXPLORE YOUR ANGER WORKSHEET

Who or what triggered the anger reaction?

What does anger want to say? Record it or write it down as you express it.

What words or interactions allowed anger to present itself?

Where do you feel anger? Scan your body from your big toe to your head if you're unsure.

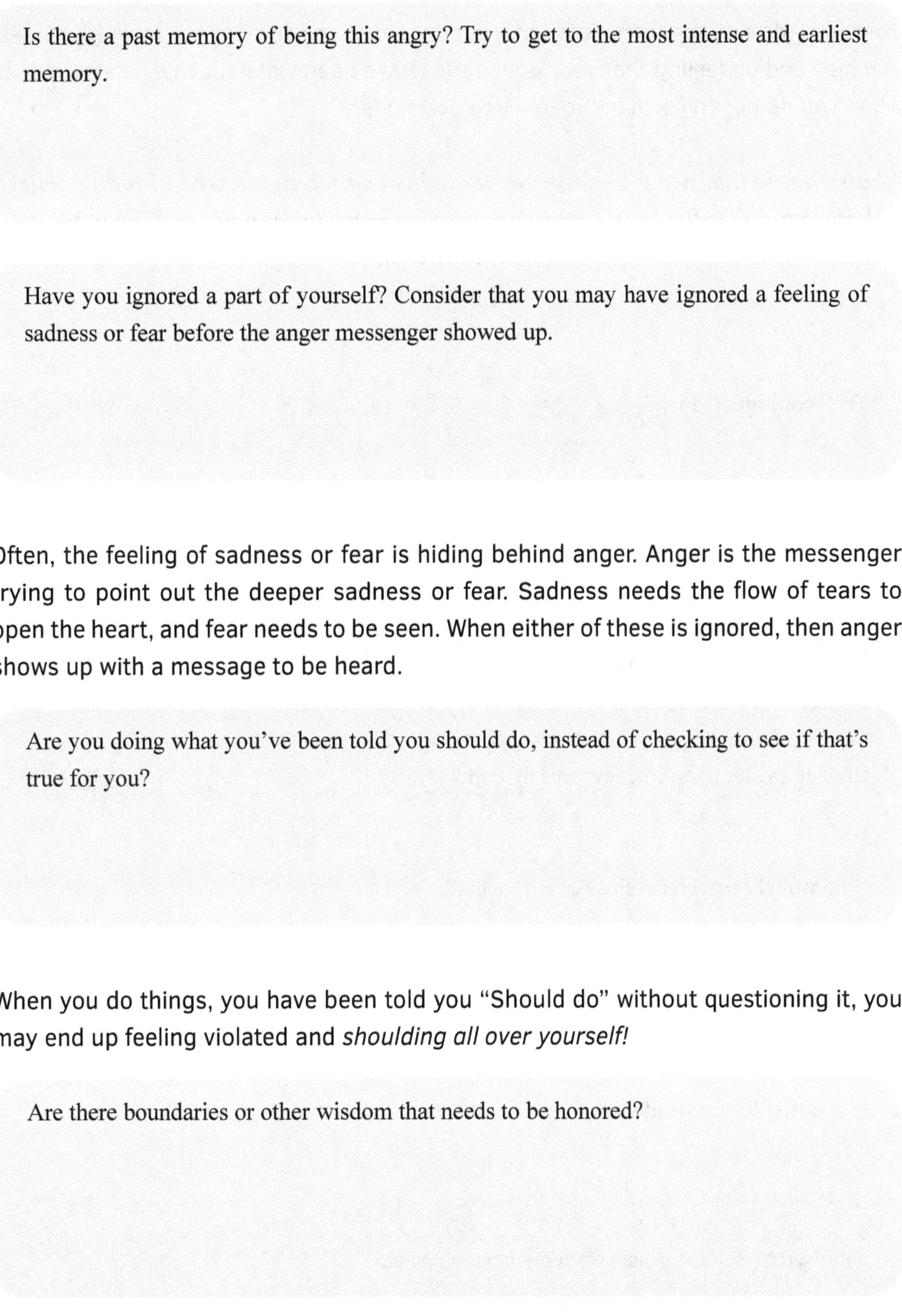

Is there a past memory of being this angry? Try to get to the most intense and earliest memory.

Have you ignored a part of yourself? Consider that you may have ignored a feeling of sadness or fear before the anger messenger showed up.

Often, the feeling of sadness or fear is hiding behind anger. Anger is the messenger trying to point out the deeper sadness or fear. Sadness needs the flow of tears to open the heart, and fear needs to be seen. When either of these is ignored, then anger shows up with a message to be heard.

Are you doing what you've been told you should do, instead of checking to see if that's true for you?

When you do things, you have been told you "Should do" without questioning it, you may end up feeling violated and *shoulding all over yourself!*

Are there boundaries or other wisdom that needs to be honored?

When you do not question situations, actions, etc., and truly check in with yourself, you may end up feeling that your boundaries have been violated. You violate yourself when you do not check in before making decisions.

"I discovered that when I believe my thoughts I suffered, but when I didn't believe them, I didn't suffer, and that this is true for every human being. Freedom is as simple as that."
-Byron Katie

The Fear I ignored is:

I looked at my fear directly and asked:
Is it true?

How do I know for certain it's true?

How do I react when I believe this thought?

Who would I be without this belief/thought?

See The Work by Byron Katie

I acknowledged my sadness of:

I allowed myself to cry and open my heart channel.

After a good cry I feel:

My messenger of anger pointed out _______________________________________

____

Showing up in the ____part of my body.

I ignored the signal of fear/sadness (circle one) when_____________________________

____

I learned ____

____

I am committed to listening to the signals of fear, sadness, anger and honoring their wisdom ____ (Sign/date)

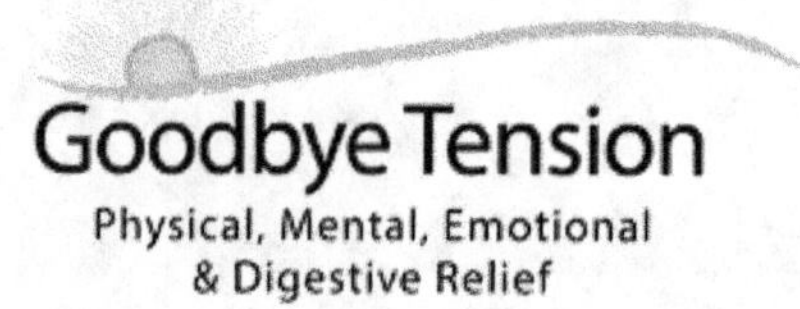

EXPLORE YOUR ANGER WORKSHEET

Who or what triggered the anger reaction?

What does anger want to say? Record it or write it down as you express it.

What words or interactions allowed anger to present itself?

Where do you feel anger? Scan your body from your big toe to your head if you're unsure.

Is there a past memory of being this angry? Try to get to the most intense and earliest memory.

Have you ignored a part of yourself? Consider that you may have ignored a feeling of sadness or fear before the anger messenger showed up.

Often, the feeling of sadness or fear is hiding behind anger. Anger is the messenger trying to point out the deeper sadness or fear. Sadness needs the flow of tears to open the heart, and fear needs to be seen. When either of these is ignored, then anger shows up with a message to be heard.

Are you doing what you've been told you should do, instead of checking to see if that's true for you?

When you do things, you have been told you "Should do" without questioning it, you may end up feeling violated and *shoulding all over yourself!*

Are there boundaries or other wisdom that needs to be honored?

When you do not question situations, actions, etc., and truly check in with yourself, you may end up feeling that your boundaries have been violated. You violate yourself when you do not check in before making decisions.

"I discovered that when I believe my thoughts I suffered, but when I didn't believe them, I didn't suffer, and that this is true for every human being. Freedom is as simple as that."
-Byron Katie

The Fear I ignored is:

I looked at my fear directly and asked:
Is it true?

How do I know for certain it's true?

How do I react when I believe this thought?

Who would I be without this belief/thought?

See The Work by Byron Katie

I acknowledged my sadness of:

I allowed myself to cry and open my heart channel.

After a good cry I feel:

My messenger of anger pointed out _______________________________________

____

Showing up in the ____part of my body.

I ignored the signal of fear/sadness (circle one) when____________________________

____

I learned ____

____

I am committed to listening to the signals of fear, sadness, anger and honoring their wisdom ____ (Sign/date)

EXPLORE YOUR ANGER WORKSHEET

Who or what triggered the anger reaction?

What does anger want to say? Record it or write it down as you express it.

What words or interactions allowed anger to present itself?

Where do you feel anger? Scan your body from your big toe to your head if you're unsure.

Is there a past memory of being this angry? Try to get to the most intense and earliest memory.

Have you ignored a part of yourself? Consider that you may have ignored a feeling of sadness or fear before the anger messenger showed up.

Often, the feeling of sadness or fear is hiding behind anger. Anger is the messenger trying to point out the deeper sadness or fear. Sadness needs the flow of tears to open the heart, and fear needs to be seen. When either of these is ignored, then anger shows up with a message to be heard.

Are you doing what you've been told you should do, instead of checking to see if that's true for you?

When you do things, you have been told you "Should do" without questioning it, you may end up feeling violated and *shoulding all over yourself!*

Are there boundaries or other wisdom that needs to be honored?

When you do not question situations, actions, etc., and truly check in with yourself, you may end up feeling that your boundaries have been violated. You violate yourself when you do not check in before making decisions.

"I discovered that when I believe my thoughts I suffered, but when I didn't believe them, I didn't suffer, and that this is true for every human being. Freedom is as simple as that."
-Byron Katie

The Fear I ignored is:

I looked at my fear directly and asked:
Is it true?

How do I know for certain it's true?

How do I react when I believe this thought?

Who would I be without this belief/thought?

See The Work by Byron Katie

I acknowledged my sadness of:

I allowed myself to cry and open my heart channel.

After a good cry I feel:

My messenger of anger pointed out ____________________________________
____
Showing up in the ____part of my body.
I ignored the signal of fear/sadness (circle one) when____________________________
____
I learned ____
____
I am committed to listening to the signals of fear, sadness, anger and honoring their wisdom ____ (Sign/date)

DAILY SELF-CARE TRACKER

DATE: **I WOKE AT:**

UPON WAKING I FEEL...

Breathing Practice

Type:

How long:

Movement Exercise

Type:

How long:

Breakfast

When:

What:

Water

Quantity:

Temp:

What was the best part of the morning?

How would I have preferred the morning been?

What can I change within for a better experience?

MID-DAY I FEEL....

Breathing Practice

Type:

How long:

Work/Study

Lunch

When:

What:

Water

Quantity:

Temp:

What was the best part of the afternoon?

How would I have preferred the afternoon been?

What can I change within for a better experience?

EVENING I FEEL...

Breathing Practice

Type:

How long:

Chores

Dinner

When:

What:

Water

Quantity:

Temp:

What was the best part of the evening?

How would I have preferred the evening been?

What can I change within for a better experience?

Did I resolve my emotions, experiences, & perceptions using the EDHIR® process or the I'm TRIGGERED! Pocket guide?
Explain:

PREPARING FOR SLEEP I FEEL...

Breathing Practice	**Self-Care**
Type:	Type:
How long:	Went to sleep at:

DAILY SELF-CARE TRACKER

DATE: **I WOKE AT:**

UPON WAKING I FEEL...

Breathing Practice	**Movement Exercise**	**Breakfast**	**Water**
Type:	Type:	When:	Quantity:
How long:	How long:	What:	Temp:

What was the best part of the morning?

How would I have preferred the morning been?

What can I change within for a better experience?

MID-DAY I FEEL....

Breathing Practice

Type:

How long:

Work/Study

Lunch

When:

What:

Water

Quantity:

Temp:

What was the best part of the afternoon?

How would I have preferred the afternoon been?

What can I change within for a better experience?

EVENING I FEEL...

Breathing Practice

Type:

How long:

Chores

Dinner

When:

What:

Water

Quantity:

Temp:

What was the best part of the evening?

How would I have preferred the evening been?

What can I change within for a better experience?

Did I resolve my emotions, experiences, & perceptions using the EDHIR® process or the I'm TRIGGERED! Pocket guide?
Explain:

PREPARING FOR SLEEP I FEEL...

Breathing Practice
Type:

How long:

Self-Care
Type:

Went to sleep at:

DAILY SELF-CARE TRACKER

DATE: **I WOKE AT:**

UPON WAKING I FEEL...

Breathing Practice

Type:

How long:

Movement Exercise

Type:

How long:

Breakfast

When:

What:

Water

Quantity:

Temp:

What was the best part of the morning?

How would I have preferred the morning been?

What can I change within for a better experience?

MID-DAY I FEEL....

Breathing Practice
Type:

How long:

Work/Study

Lunch
When:

What:

Water
Quantity:

Temp:

What was the best part of the afternoon?

How would I have preferred the afternoon been?

What can I change within for a better experience?

EVENING I FEEL...

Breathing Practice
Type:

How long:

Chores

Dinner
When:

What:

Water
Quantity:

Temp:

What was the best part of the evening?

How would I have preferred the evening been?

What can I change within for a better experience?

Did I resolve my emotions, experiences, & perceptions using the EDHIR® process or the I'm TRIGGERED! Pocket guide?
Explain:

PREPARING FOR SLEEP I FEEL...

Breathing Practice
Type:

How long:

Self-Care
Type:

Went to sleep at:

ABOUT THE AUTHOR

Jeannine Rashidi is a highly qualified health and wellness practitioner. She opened her Goodbye Tension practice in 2003, focused on alleviating the core of physical, digestive, emotional, and mental tension. Her commitment to empower and inspire her clients toward awakening the healer within has been a passion for the last 18 years. She also brings her personal experiences of healing trauma, including the EDHIR® process she created to guide her clients toward integrating the Heart and Mind after the disconnect from trauma and adverse life experiences. Jeannine is also an Ayurvedic Practitioner finishing her last year in the Ayurvedic Doctorate program at Kerala Ayurveda Academy. She has apprenticed under Dr. Jayarajan Kodikannath since 2016, traveled to Kerala to directly experience the roots of Ayurveda, and is an ongoing Samskritam (Sanskrit) student to enable her to study the source Ayurvedic books directly. Jeannine is a devoted wife, mother, and recent grandmother. In her spare time, she enjoys cooking, photography, meditation, time dedicated to family, spiritual practice, and creating stories with gnomes, and other fairytale creatures, continuing the tradition from her late grandmother Laurel.

INTERESTED IN WORKING TOGETHER ON YOUR HEALING JOURNEY?

ONLINE APPOINTMENTS ARE OFFERED WORLDWIDE.

INQUIRE AT GOODBYETENSION.COM
OR
EMAIL: BYETENSION@GMAIL.COM